THE MOVIE BOOK

OF ANSWERS®

THE MOVIE BOOK
OF ANSWERS®

CAROL BOLT

NEW YORK

LIBRARY OF CONGRESS CATALOGING-IN-PUBLICATION DATA

BOLT, CAROL, 1963–
    THE MOVIE BOOK OF ANSWERS / CAROL BOLT.—1ST ED.
    P. CM.
    ISBN 0-7868-6700-0
    1. FORTUNE-TELLING BY BOOKS. 2. MOTION PICTURES—QUOTATIONS, MAXIMS, ETC.
I. TITLE

BF1891.B66 B 65 2001
133.3—DC21

                                                          2001024758

FIRST EDITION

10 9 8 7 6 5 4 3 2 1

How to Use
The Movie Book of Answers®

1. Hold the **closed** book in your hand, on your lap, or on a table.

2. Take 10 or 15 seconds to **concentrate** on your question. Questions should be phrased **closed-end**, e.g., "Is the Job I'm Applying for the Right One?" or "Should I Travel this Weekend?"

3. While visualizing or speaking your question (one question at a time), place **one hand** palm down on the book's front cover and **stroke the edge** of the pages, back to front.

4. When you **sense** the time is right, **open** the book and there will be your answer.

5. **Repeat** the process for as many questions as you have.

Got questions? This book has the answers.

Carol Bolt is a professional artist living in Seattle. She is also the author of *The Book of Answers®* and *The Literary Book of Answers®*.

200522

THE MOVIE BOOK
OF ANSWERS®

BRAG ABOUT IT.

—Sam Spade: *The Maltese Falcon*

BAA-RAM-EWE.
TO YOUR OWN BREED,
YOUR FLEECE,
YOUR CLAN BE TRUE.

—Sheep: *Babe*

[DON'T] LET IT GET AWAY.

—Oscar: *Sweet Charity*

IT'S A REAL BAD WIND THAT DON'T BLOW SOMEBODY SOME GOOD.

—Senator Oliver Whiteside: *Giant*

FASTEN YOUR SEAT BELTS— IT'S GOING TO BE A BUMPY NIGHT.

—Margo Channing: *All About Eve*

TO SURVIVE
ONE MUST HAVE
A PLAN.

—Willie: *Lifeboat*

YOU GOTTA DRAW AND FIRE FASTER THAN SOMEBODY ELSE.

—Cole Thorton: *The Road to El Dorado*

AH, SWEET MYSTERY OF LIFE AT LAST [YOU] FOUND [IT]!

—Elizabeth: *Young Frankenstein*

[BE] READY FOR
[YOUR] CLOSE-UP.

—Norma Desmond: *Sunset Boulevard*

DON'T DO ANYTHING HASTY.

—Angela Vickers: *A Place in the Sun*

IT'S NOT IN [YOUR] HANDS.

—Maggie: *City of Angels*

DO YOU HAVE THE GUTS
TO DO WHAT'S RIGHT?

—Juror #11: *12 Angry Men*

FORM MUST FOLLOW FUNCTION.

—Cameron: *The Fountainhead*

THINK BIG, ACT BIG
AND YOU'LL BE BIG.

—Tom "Ross" Finley: *Sweet Bird of Youth*

GO THOSE [LAST] MILES BEFORE IT'S TOO LATE.

—Mrs. Carrie Watts: *The Trip to Bountiful*

I GUESS THAT'S THE WAY
IT CRUMBLES . . . COOKIE-WISE.

—Fran Kubelik: *The Apartment*

IF THAT'S YOUR STORY, STICK TO IT.

—Madge: *Top Hat*

WHAT YOU SAY COUNTS.

—Sean Thornton: *The Quiet Man*

PUT [YOUR] SHOE ON THE OTHER FOOT.

—King Marchand: *Victor/Victoria*

GET A SHOT AT IT.

—Jimmy "Popeye" Doyle: *The French Connection*

NO.

—Denys: *Out of Africa*

YOU WILL HAVE [IT]
WHEN YOU NEED IT.

—Nickie Ferrante: *An Affair to Remember*

DON'T LET TOO MUCH DEVOTION GET YOU IRRITABLE.

—Brick: *Cat on a Hot Tin Roof*

THAT'S THE WAY
THE CRACKERS CRUMBLE.

—Ruth: *A Raisin in the Sun*

BE CONTENT WITH WHAT YOU HAVE.

—Alice Tripp: *A Place in the Sun*

YOU'LL NEED A FRIEND.

—Fiedler: *The Spy Who Came in From the Cold*

SNAP OUT OF IT!

—Loretta Castorini: *Moonstruck*

IT IS A RED HERRING.

—Miss Scarlet: *Clue*

[YOU MAY] END UP BACK IN THE SAME PLACE.

—Josh Leonard: *The Blair Witch Project*

YOU SHOULDN'T LET YOURSELF ATTACH MUCH IMPORTANCE TO THESE THINGS.

—Kasper Gutman: *The Maltese Falcon*

THIS BUSINESS REQUIRES A CERTAIN AMOUNT OF FINESSE.

—Jake Gittes: *Chinatown*

JUST MAKE SURE THE HONEY STAYS IN THE HIVE.

—Joe/Josephine: *Some Like It Hot*

[IT'S] POLYMORPHOUSLY PERVERSE.

—Alvy Singer: *Annie Hall*

COPY THE MASTERS
TO LEARN THEIR SECRETS.

—Charles Bonnet: *How to Steal a Million*

WHAT ELSE COULD YA DO?

—Belle Rosen: *The Poseidon Adventure*

IT [MAY] SEEM TO SWOOP
DOWN AT YOU DELIBERATELY.

—Mitch: *The Birds*

THERE'S SOME THINGS IN THIS WORLD YOU JUST GOTTA FACE.

—Maggie: *Cat on a Hot Tin Roof*

[IT WOULD] BE CRAZY
TO IGNORE IT.

—Melanie Daniels: *The Birds*

SOMETIMES [THINGS] NEED A LOT OF WATCHING.

—Sergeant Jack Graham: *Shadow of a Doubt*

THE BULLET IN [ANOTHER] GUN IS FASTER THAN YOURS.

—Lee: *The Magnificent Seven*

YES.

—Shanghai Lily: *Shanghai Express*

[YOU] CAN MAKE IT IF YOU RUN.

—Dr. Ellie Sattler: *Jurassic Park*

REASSEMBLE YOUR FACULTIES AND START PACKING.

—Phileas Fogg: *Around the World In 80 Days*

SIT HERE
AND BE QUIET.

—Mrs. Bates: *Psycho*

SOME PEOPLE [WOULD]
PAY A LOT OF MONEY
FOR THAT INFORMATION.

—Michael Corleone: *The Godfather*

ONE'S TOO MANY AND A HUNDRED'S NOT ENOUGH.

—Nat: *The Lost Weekend*

NOBODY'S GONNA RAIN ON [YOUR] PARADE.

—Fanny Brice: *Funny Girl*

[DON'T] LET [YOUR]
GOLDEN MOMENT
PASS [YOU] BY.

—Billy: *Carousel*

GO WITH THE FLOW.

—Dr. Michaels: *Fantastic Voyage*

[YOU] CAN'T HELP [YOUR]SELF.

—Larry Talbot/Wolf Man: *The Wolf Man*

IT'S PERFECT.

—Joanna Eberhart: *The Stepford Wives*

REVEL IN YOUR TIME.

—Eldon Tyrell: *Blade Runner*

KEEP IN TOUCH WITH ALL THE LOOSE ENDS.

—Sam Spade: *The Maltese Falcon*

IT WOULD BE
BAD MANNERS TO TELL.

—Dorothy Parker:
Mrs. Parker and the Vicious Circle

IT IS A GUARANTEE OF
YOUR IMPARTIALITY THAT
YOU DO NOT KNOW.

—Soviet Intelligence Officer:
The Spy Who Came in From the Cold

[BE] HIP ABOUT TIME.

—Captain America: *Easy Rider*

[DON'T] BEG FOR A RIDE
THAT'LL TAKE [YOU] BACK
TO WHERE [YOU] STARTED.

—Cora Smith:
The Postman Always Rings Twice

SUCCESS OR FAILURE WILL DEPEND ENTIRELY UPON YOU.

—Principal: *To Sir, with Love*

MAKE TIME.

—Frank Stark: *Rebel Without a Cause*

THE LONGER YOU WAIT
THE MORE SENSE YOU GET.

—Jerry: *The Divorcee*

WANT NO PART OF THAT BULL; EXCEPT ON A PLATE MEDIUM RARE.

—Gay: *The Misfits*

MOVE ON.

—Adelaide: *The Turning Point*

WHAD' [ELSE] YA GOT THERE IN YER POKE?

—Rooster Cogburn: *True Grit*

DON'T DILLYDALLY.

—Phileas Fogg:
Around the World in 80 Days

WHAT'S THE DIFFERENCE?

—Terry: *The Dark Mirror*

IT'S GOT TO BE CONVINCING.

—Tony: *Dial M for Murder*

STAY DOWN AND
LOOK FOR BIG HATS.

—Pike Bishop: *The Wild Bunch*

TAKE IT EASY, BUT TAKE IT.

—Radio Announcer: *Midnight Cowboy*

WHOA.

—Velvet Brown: *National Velvet*

[DON'T] USE A BULLDOZER TO FIND A CHINA CUP.

—Belloq: *Raiders of the Lost Ark*

THERE'LL BE NO ONE
TO STOP [YOU].

—Darth Vader: *Star Wars*

DON'T MAKE A BIT OF SENSE TO ME.

—Randle Patrick McMurphy:
One Flew Over the Cuckoo's Nest

YOU GOTTA FIND A WAY
TO MAKE IT WORK.

—George Fields: *Tootsie*

[YOU] CAN NEVER GO BACK.

—Narrator: *Rebecca*

I SUGGEST YOU
GET ON WITH IT.

—Ethel: *On Golden Pond*

NO[BODY] SHOULD KNOW
TOO MUCH
ABOUT HIS OWN DESTINY.

—Doc Brown:
Back to the Future

IF YOU BUILD IT, [THEY] WILL COME.

—Voice in Cornfield:
Field of Dreams

EITHER LEAD [THIS] BUNCH
OR END IT RIGHT NOW.

—Pike Bishop: *The Wild Bunch*

A TANTALIZING PLUM HAS DROPPED INTO [YOUR] LAP.

—Carol Lipton:
Manhattan Murder Mystery

THE CALENDAR TAKES CARE OF EVERYTHING.

—Maerose: *Prizzi's Honor*

LOOKS LIKE IT'S GONNA BE A
LONGER ONE THAN YOU FIGURED.

—Sergeant Sefton: *Stalag 17*

THERE'S NO PLACE LIKE HOME.

—Glinda, the Good Witch:
The Wizard of Oz

[IT'S NOT] GONNA JUST JUMP INTO THE BOAT.

—Norman: *On Golden Pond*

YOU PAYS YER MONEY,
YOU TAKES YER CHOICE.

—Charlie: *The African Queen*

DEFINE THAT.

—Will Hunting: *Good Will Hunting*

NO.

—Mrs. Bates: *Psycho*

DON'T GO ALONE.

—Steve: *Singles*

THIS [COULD]
SWALLOW YOU WHOLE.
NO SHAKIN', NO TENDERIZIN',
DOWN YOU GO
[SO YOU] GOTTA DO IT QUICK.

—Quint: *Jaws*

WORK ALONE.

—Serpico: *Serpico*

AYUH.

—Billy: *Carousel*

TURN A DEFEAT INTO VICTORY.

—Colonel Nicholson:
The Bridge on the River Kwai

ONCE YOU HAVE FOUND [IT] NEVER LET [IT] GO.

—Emile: *South Pacific*

DON'T CHOKE NOW, IT'S NOT THAT HARD A SHOT.

—Vincent: *The Color of Money*

[HAVE] JUST AS MANY
NOTES AS REQUIRED;
NO MORE, NO LESS.

—Mozart: *Amadeus*

[YOU] CAN'T WALK AWAY
FROM IT.

—Frank Bullitt: *Bullitt*

YOU CAN'T HAVE IT TWO WAYS.

—Doris Attinger: *Adam's Rib*

WHATEVER.

—Amber: *Clueless*

YOU'RE GONNA NEED A BIGGER BOAT.

—Brody: *Jaws*

SEE WHERE IT LEADS.

—Colonel Mustard: *Clue*

I'VE WARNED YOU FAIRLY, DON'T CHANGE YOUR COURSE.

—Faith Wishart: *Ebb Tide*

IN A MOST DELIGHTFUL WAY.

—Mary Poppins: *Mary Poppins*

LOOK FOR THE
BEAR NECESSITIES.

—Baloo the Bear: *The Jungle Book*

THE FUTURE IS NOT SET.

—Kyle Reese: *The Terminator*

[YOU] GOT NO STRINGS TO HOLD [YOU] DOWN.

—Pinocchio: *Pinocchio*

TAKE ALL THE PIECES,
PUT THEM TOGETHER
ONE BY ONE.

—Inspector Peterson: *Mildred Pierce*

[THAT'S] QUITE A PARCEL.

—Dr. Horace Lynnton: *Giant*

[DON'T] SAY THAT LIKE IT'S A NEGATIVE THING.

—Alvy Singer: *Annie Hall*

ALL THIS COMES UP UNDER THE HEADING OF ADVENTURE.

—George Conway: *Lost Horizon*

SOME THINGS;
ONCE THEY'RE DONE,
CAN'T BE UNDONE.

—Ted: *Kramer vs. Kramer*

IT COULD WORK.

—Dr. Frederick Frankenstein: *Young Frankenstein*

REMEMBER THE LITTLE THINGS.

—Charlie Babbitt: *Rain Man*

ACKNOWLEDGE YOUR RESPONSIBILITIES.

—Alex: *Fatal Attraction*

STAY ON TARGET.

—Fighter Pilot Gold #5: *Star Wars*

THIS [WILL BE] SOMETHING OF AN EXPEDITION.

—Col. Harry Brighton: *Lawrence of Arabia*

YOU TELL ME WHAT YOU KNOW AND I'LL CONFIRM.

—Deep Throat: *All the President's Men*

YOU HAVE TO SAY SAYONARA.

—Radio Voice from Seoul: M*A*S*H

YES.

—Count Dracula: *Dracula*

PLAY ACCORDING TO YOUR RULES.

—Jedediah Leland: *Citizen Kane*

[GET IT] IN THE LARGE ECONOMY SIZE.

—Joe: *Tarantula*

IT MAKES PERFECT SENSE.

—Agent J: *Men in Black*

IT'S THE BIGGEST THING IN THE WORLD.

—Carl Denham: *King Kong*

MORE, MORE, MORE.

—Janet: *The Rocky Horror Picture Show*

SPEN[D] A LOT OF TIME
SETTIN' THIS ONE UP.

—Sal: *The French Connection*

THE WHOLE POINT IS LOST
IF YOU KEEP IT A SECRET.

—Dr. Strangelove:
Dr. Strangelove or: How I Learned to
Stop Worrying and
Love the Bomb

KEEP GOING.

—Thelma Dickinson: *Thelma & Louise*

ALWAYS BE CLOSING.

—Blake: *Glengarry Glen Ross*

RELAX, DAMMIT, RELAX.

—Oscar: *The Odd Couple*

GO FROM THIS PLACE.

—Commander of the Hosts:
The Ten Commandments

JUST FOLLOW
THE YELLOW BRICK ROAD.

—Glinda, the Good Witch:
The Wizard of Oz

IT'LL PROBABLY TURN OUT TO BE A VERY SIMPLE THING.

—Mr. Rawlston: *Citizen Kane*

[YOU] HAVE SUCH
A GOOD CHANCE.

—Atticus Finch: *To Kill a Mockingbird*

THAT'S THE SITUATION
AND THE BOX IT CAME IN.

—Mrs. Marion Kerby: *Topper*

PHONE HOME.

—E.T.: E.T. The Extra-Terrestrial

FRANKLY MY DEAR, [YOU] DON'T GIVE A DAMN.

—Rhett Butler: *Gone with the Wind*

MAYBE NOT TODAY.
MAYBE NOT TOMORROW,
BUT SOON.

—Rick: *Casablanca*

TAKE IT EASY, YOU'LL LIVE LONGER.

—Sal: *Do the Right Thing*

GO OUT THE WAY [YOU] CAME IN.

—Helen Lawson: *Valley of the Dolls*

SEE THE RACE TO ITS END.

—Eric Liddell: *Chariots of Fire*

CONTROL YOURSELF PUBLIC-WISE.

—Alex: *A Clockwork Orange*

THE FORCE
WILL BE WITH YOU.
ALWAYS.

—Ben (Obi-Wan) Kenobi: *Star Wars*

EXPECT THE BEST.

—Debbie: *Singles*

NOT ANYMORE.

—Blanche Hudson:
What Ever Happened to Baby Jane?

STRETCH A DOUBLE
INTO A TRIPLE.

—Archie "Moonlight" Graham:
Field of Dreams

[IT'S] LIKE
A BOX OF CHOCOLATES,
YOU NEVER KNOW WHAT
YOU'RE GONNA GET.

—Forrest Gump: *Forrest Gump*

MONEY MAKES THE
WORLD GO 'ROUND.

—Sally Bowles & Master of Ceremonies: *Cabaret*

WHEN ARE [YOU] GONNA HAVE SOME FUN?

—Oscar: *The Odd Couple*

SOMETHING [MAY] ATTACH ITSELF TO [YOU].

—Dallas: *Alien*

IT LEADS EVERYWHERE; THERE'S MORE.

—Deep Throat: *All the President's Men*

YOU'RE GOING TO HAVE TO SHARE THIS PARTY LINE.

—Jan Morrow: *Pillow Talk*

THE THING AIN'T THE RING, IT'S THE PLAY.

—Jake LaMotta: *Raging Bull*

STICK TO
ESTABLISHED PROCEDURES.

—Dr. Jeremy Stone: *The Andromeda Strain*

IT SOUNDS BETTER IN FRENCH.

—Jerry Mulligan: *An American in Paris*

ALL MY READINGS POINT TO SOMETHING BIG ON THE HORIZON.

—Dr. Egon Spengler: *Ghostbusters*

HEIGH-HO, HEIGH-HO, IT'S HOME FROM WORK [YOU] GO.

—Seven Dwarfs: *Snow White and the Seven Dwarfs*

MAKE AN OFFER
[THEY] CAN'T REFUSE.

—Michael Corleone: *The Godfather*

[SOMETIMES] BEING BAD FEELS PRETTY GOOD.

—John Bender: *The Breakfast Club*

THERE IS NOTHING CASUAL ABOUT IT.

—Guy Holden: *The Gay Divorcee*

[GO] TO THE PUPPET SHOW,
SEE THE STRINGS.

—Rod Tidwell: *Jerry Maguire*

LET'S CUT THIS SHORT.

—Otis B. Driftwood:
A Night at the Opera

SEE WHAT THE MAJORITY THINKS.

—Max Bialystock: *The Producers*

ALL THERE REALLY IS,
IS THE NEXT THING
THAT HAPPENS.

—Roslyn: *The Misfits*

THERE WON'T BE ANY TROUBLE IF YOU RIDE ON.

—Chris Adams: *The Magnificent Seven*

IT REQUIRES SOME SPECIAL QUALITY OF EFFORT.

—Monsignor Ryan: *Guess Who's Coming to Dinner*

[YOU] GOT SO MUCH; GIVE SOME AWAY.

—Charity Hope Valentine: *Sweet Charity*

[BETTER TO] HAVE
THIRTY MINUTES OF
SOMETHING WONDERFUL
THAN A LIFETIME OF
NOTHING SPECIAL.

—Shelby: *Steel Magnolias*

DON'T GET IN THE WAY.

—Jesus Christ: *The Last Temptation of Christ*

YOU MUST LOVE THE DOING.

—Roark: *The Fountainhead*

KEEP IT ALL TO YOURSELF.

—Stanley: *The Conversation*

ANYTHING YOU DO COULD HAVE SERIOUS REPERCUSSIONS ON FUTURE EVENTS.

—Doc Brown: *Back to the Future*

BITCHIN'.

—Jeff Spicoli: *Fast Times at Ridgemont High*

FIND [YOUR] OWN SHANGRI-LA.

—Mr. Gainsford: *Lost Horizon*

YOU LOOK STRONG ENOUGH.

—Moses: *The Ten Commandments*

MY GOODNESS, [WOULDN'T] IT HELP?

—Lorelei Lee: *Gentlemen Prefer Blondes*

[YOU] WAS BORN GAME.

—Rooster Cogburn: *True Grit*

STOP OFF FOR A QUICK ONE EN ROUTE.

—James Bond: *Goldfinger*

STAY COOL.

—John Milner: *American Graffiti*

THERE'S ALWAYS A MAN FASTER ON THE DRAW THAN YOU ARE.

—Wyatt Earp: *Gunfight at the O.K. Corral*

[IT'S] NOT ABOUT THE DETAILS. IT'S ABOUT THE BIG PICTURE.

—Ed Wood: *Ed Wood*

PLAY AS WELL AS YOU CAN;
OTHERWISE YOU GOT
NOTHING TO TALK ABOUT
IN THE LOCKER ROOM.

—Maude: *Harold and Maude*

HAVE A WONDERFUL TIME, WHOEVER [YOU'RE] WITH.

—Elwood P. Dowd: *Harvey*

[THAT'S] A TARGET-RICH ENVIRONMENT.

—Maverick: *Top Gun*

THAT'S THE NEXT PLACE TO WATCH.

—L.B. Jeffries: *Rear Window*

FIND A REAL LIFE [THING]
THAT MAKES [YOU] FEEL
LIKE TIFFANY'S.

—Holly Golightly: *Breakfast at Tiffany's*

I DON'T THINK YOU OUGHT TO MAKE ANY MORE OF IT.

—Dr. Danny Kauffman:
Invasion of the Body Snatchers

IF YOU WANT IT,
THROW A LASSO AROUND IT
AND PULL IT DOWN.

—George Bailey: *It's a Wonderful Life*

I DON'T HAVE ANYTHING BRILLIANT, I ONLY KNOW AS MUCH AS YOU DO.

—Juror #8: *12 Angry Men*

[YOU] HAVE NOTHING TO LOSE.

—Lester Burnham: *American Beauty*

KEEP [Y]OUR MIND OPEN TO ANYTHING.

—Colonel Tom Edwards: *Plan 9 from Outer Space*

BE [A] GOOD NEIGHBOR.

—Police Officer: *Manhattan Murder Mystery*

GET OUT OF TOWN AND REALLY LET [Y]OUR HAIR DOWN.

—Thelma Dickinson: *Thelma & Louise*

SOMETIMES YOU GOTTA LOSE YOURSELF 'FORE YOU CAN FIND ANYTHING.

—Lewis Medlock: *Deliverance*

YOU GET WHAT YOU SETTLE FOR.

—Louise Sawyer: *Thelma & Louise*

DO YA FEEL LUCKY?
WELL, DO YA . . . ?

—Harry Callahan: *Dirty Harry*

HAVE SOMETHING TO FALL BACK ON OTHER THAN YOUR ASS.

—Bob: *My Own Private Idaho*

[YOU MAY] NOT BE ABLE
TO [DO] IT IN THE DARK.

—Heather Donahue: *The Blair Witch Project*

IT [COULD] BE BOGUS.

—Duckie: *Pretty in Pink*

OH YES, YOU CAN

. . . YOU MUST.

—Captain Von Trapp: *The Sound of Music*

GO WHILE THE GOIN'S GOOD.

—Charlie: *The African Queen*

SHOW [THEM] WHAT YOU'RE MADE OF.

—Roy Batty: *Blade Runner*

IT'S GONNA BE LIKE
MONEY FROM HOME.

—Joe Buck: *Midnight Cowboy*

SEE WHO'S AROUND.

—Father Dyer: *The Exorcist*

PUT [IT] IN YOUR POCKET.

—Tracy Lord: *The Philadelphia Story*

CHOOSE A LOVELY SPOT
FOR [THE] MEETING.

—Karen Holmes: *From Here to Eternity*

[REMEMBER] THERE'S A
GREAT BIG HUNK OF WORLD
OUT THERE WITH NO FENCE
AROUND IT.

—Tramp: *Lady and the Tramp*

DEPEND ON THE
KINDNESS OF STRANGERS.

—Blanche Dubois: *A Streetcar Named Desire*

YOU'VE GOT
SECURITY CLEARANCE.

—Maverick: *Top Gun*

A LITTLE DAB'LL DO YA.

—Randle Patrick McMurphy:
One Flew Over the Cuckoo's Nest

YOU'RE DARNED TOOTIN'.

—Jerry Lundegaard: *Fargo*

YEAH BUT [DON'T BE] SO
PREOCCUPIED WITH WHETHER
OR NOT [YOU] COULD . . .
STOP TO THINK IF [YOU]
SHOULD.

—Dr. Ian Malcolm: *Jurassic Park*

MAKE SURE IT'S KNOWN.

—Oskar Schindler: *Schindler's List*

[YOU'RE] NOT GONNA WANNA LOAD THE BASES.

—Shoeless Joe Jackson: *Field of Dreams*

GO THE DISTANCE.

—Rocky Balboa: *Rocky*

KICK OFF YOUR SPURS.

—Leslie Lynnton Benedict: *Giant*

CONSIDER THINGS FROM [ANOTHER'S] POINT OF VIEW.

—Atticus Finch: *To Kill a Mockingbird*

IT'S NOTHING LIKE YOU'VE
EVER GONE AFTER BEFORE.

—Marcus Brody: *Raiders of the Lost Ark*

STAY OUT OF TROUBLE.

—Robocop: *Robocop*

BE HAPPY IN YOUR WORK.

—Colonel Saito: *The Bridge on the River Kwai*

[YOU] COULD DO DEEZ T'INGS.

—Tony Manero: *Saturday Night Fever*

GIVE IT UP.

—Dash Hammett: *Julia*

IF YOU GOTTA GO, GO WITH A SMILE.

—The Joker: *Batman*

KEEP YOUR SWORDS BRIGHT.

—Sheik Ilderim

AND YOUR INTENTIONS TRUE.

—Judah
Ben-Hur

YOU CAN'T SWITCH
TO ANOTHER STATION.

—Max Schumacher: *Network*

YES, BUT DON'T HOLD THAT AGAINST ME.

—Peter Warne: *It Happened One Night*

DO SOMETHIN' BIGGER.

—Lena: *A Raisin in the Sun*

SEPARATE THE FACTS
FROM THE FANCY.

—Judge: *12 Angry Men*

LAY OFF THE STUFF FOR AWHILE.

—Nat: *The Lost Weekend*

IT HAS TO COME NATURALLY.

—Victoria: *Victor/Victoria*

THERE ARE OTHERS.

—Helen St. James: *The Lost Weekend*

[YOU] CAN MAKE A GREAT STATE
FROM A LITTLE CITY.

—T. E. Lawrence: *Lawrence of Arabia*

GET CLOSER [TO IT].

—**Dr. Hannibal Lecter:** *The Silence of the Lambs*

LOOK IN FRONT OF YOU.

—Jack Griffin: *The Invisible Man*

YOU GOTTA GO WHERE THINGS HAPPEN.

—Dave Hooch: *A League of Their Own*

[YOUR] AFFILIATES WON'T CARRY [YOU].

—Nelson Chaney: *Network*

KEEP IT BIG.

—Jordan "Bick" Benedict: *Giant*

MAKE YOUR MOVE.

—Joel Goodson: *Risky Business*

TAKE NOTHING BUT THE BEST.

—Tramp: *Lady and the Tramp*

[YOU] [W]ON'T WANT
CONVENTIONAL PROGRAMMING.

—Diana Christensen: *Network*

[YOU] WOULDN'T BE MUCH USE WITHOUT [IT].

—George Baines: *The Piano*

PROTECT YOURSELF.

—Serpico: *Serpico*

YES . . . YES, YES, YES, YES,
YEEESSS . . . OOHHH . . .
YES, YES, YES!

—Sally: *When Harry Met Sally*

DON'T WORRY 'BOUT NUTTIN'.

—Tony Manero: *Saturday Night Fever*

PLAY IT BY THE BOOK FROM NOW ON.

—Captain Sam Bennett: *Bullitt*

DO SOMETHING TO HELP.

—Helen Cooper:
Night of the Living Dead

HEIGH-HO, HEIGH-HO, IT'S OFF TO WORK [YOU] GO.

—Seven Dwarfs:
Snow White and the Seven Dwarfs

GO AFTER WHAT [YOU] WANT
TO GO AFTER, DON'T LET IT
COME AFTER [YOU].

—Margo Channing: *All About Eve*

FIND STRENGTH
IN WHAT REMAINS BEHIND.

—Deanie Loomis quoting from
William Wordsworth's poem:
Splendor in the Grass

[DON'T] IGNORE THE STRANGE AND UNUSUAL.

—Lydia Deetz: *Beetlejuice*

WELL THERE'S SOMETHING YOU DON'T SEE EVERY DAY.

—Dr. Peter Venkman: *Ghostbusters*

WOULD IT BE INCONVENIENT?

—Macauley (Mike) Connor: *The Philadelphia Story*

NO[THING]'S PERFECT.

—Osgood E. Fielding III: *Some Like It Hot*

THERE IS NO SECOND PLACE.

—Commander Mike "Viper" Metcalf: *Top Gun*

THERE ARE A LOT OF
THINGS [I'VE] NEVER SEEN
[YOU] DO BEFORE.
THAT'S NO SIGN [NOT TO]
DO 'EM.

—Eve: *The Three Faces of Eve*

CHILL.

—Love Daddy: *Do the Right Thing*

YOU'RE PEDDLIN' [THAT] FISH IN THE WRONG MARKET.

—Nick Charles: *The Thin Man*

NO.

—Jim Stark: *Rebel Without a Cause*

YES.

—Babe the Pig: *Babe*

MINIATURIZE IT.

—Dr. Duval: *Fantastic Voyage*

[IT'S] ALMOST PERFECT.

—Barton Keyes: *Double Indemnity*

DON'T TOUCH IT.

—Q: Goldfinger

SURPRISE YOURSELF.

—Lester Burnham: *American Beauty*

[YOU'VE] BEEN IN THIS TOO LONG.

—Paul: *All Quiet on the Western Front*

IT CAN MEAN EVERYTHING OR NOTHING.

—Anne: *Valley of the Dolls*

[IT IS] ONLY INTENDED
TO WHET YOUR APPETITE.

—James Bond: *The Spy Who Loved Me*

IT DOESN'T MEAN ANYTHING.

—Gregory Anton: *Gaslight*

CREATE A PLAUSIBLE DIVERSION.

—Toddy: *Victor/Victoria*

NOT TONIGHT.

—Dave: *Play Misty for Me*

DON'T LET YOUR MOUTH
GET YOUR ASS IN TROUBLE.

—John Shaft: *Shaft*

DON'T GET DISCOURAGED.

—Gay: *The Misfits*

[DON'T] INVITE
JUST ANYBODY.

—Jena: *Pretty in Pink*

WHAT'S THE SENSE IN HAVING IT ALL?

—Lester: Shampoo

REARRANGE YOUR ALLIANCES.

—George: *Who's Afraid of Virginia Woolf?*

IT'S NOT A MATTER
OF HOW MUCH.

—Joe: *Days of Wine and Roses*

GET PREPARED FOR IT.

—Adam Bonner: *Adam's Rib*

YOU CAN NEVER LOSE
WHAT IT HAS GIVEN YOU.

—Mrs. Carrie Watts: *The Trip to Bountiful*

SOME VERY STRANGE THINGS GOING ON HERE.

—Inspector Clouseau: *The Pink Panther*

SEE WHAT'S ON THE OTHER SIDE.

—Robert Conway: *Lost Horizon*

MAKE THE BEST OF IT!

—Eric "Otter" Stratton: *Animal House*

I'M NOT SAYING YOU WON'T GET YOUR HAIR MUSSED.

—Gen. Buck Turgidson:
Dr. Strangelove or: How I Learned to Stop Worrying and Love the Bomb

I'M SORRY, I DON'T HAVE ENOUGH INFORMATION.

—HAL 9000: *2001: A Space Odyssey*

EVERYTHING'S GONNA BE ALL RIGHT.

—Sharon Waters:
My Own Private Idaho

THIS IS GONNA STRIKE
A SPECIAL RAW NERVE.

—Wolfman Jack: *American Graffiti*

IT'S ONLY A MATTER OF TIME.

—Prison Guard: *Papillon*

THE WHOLE HILL [WILL] SMELL LIKE VICTORY.

—Lt. Col. Kilgore: *Apocalypse Now*

THIS IS [YOUR] MOMENT.

—Aurora Greenaway: *Terms of Endearment*

SIT THERE QUIETLY
AND COOPERATE.

—Mrs. Iselin: *The Manchurian Candidate*

KEEP ALL YOUR HOMINY GRITS GOIN' IN THE RIGHT DIRECTION.

—Beauregard Burnside: *Auntie Mame*

GET ANOTHER SOURCE.

—Howard Simons: *All the President's Men*

TOO BAD IT CAN'T STAY
LIKE THAT ALL THE TIME.

—Johnny: *The Outsiders*

ALL GOOD THINGS TO THOSE WHO WAIT.

—Dr. Hannibal Lecter: *The Silence of the Lambs*

IT IS OBVIOUS FROM YOUR FACE
THAT YOU KNEW THE ANSWER.

—Professor Biesenthal: *Marathon Man*

S'WONDERFUL, S'MARVELOUS.

—Jerry Mulligan: *An American in Paris*

WITH [THIS]
GOES RESPONSIBILITY
TO YOURSELF AND TO OTHERS.

—Mr. Gruffydd: *How Green Was My Valley*

NOTHING'LL DO BUT YOUR OWN SWEAT AND MUSCLE.

—Joe Starrett: *Shane*

THINGS ARE GOING TO CHANGE.

—Carrie: *Carrie*

YOU MUST BE, OH SO SMART,
OR OH SO PLEASANT . . .
I RECOMMEND PLEASANT.

—Elwood P. Dowd: *Harvey*

THERE'S NOTHING TO IT.

—Linda Barrett: *Fast Times at Ridgemont High*

SOME THINGS ARE TRUE WHETHER YOU BELIEVE THEM OR NOT.

—Seth: *City of Angels*

[YOU] COULD DO IT BLINDFOLDED.

—Factory Worker: *Modern Times*

LOOK AT EVERYTHING UPSIDE DOWN.

—David Huxley: *Bringing up Baby*

SEE IF YOU LIKE IT.

—Donald: *Alice Doesn't Live Here Anymore*

IT'S HEAVY.

—Alisdair Stewart: *The Piano*

WHAT IS IT YOU'RE LOOKING FOR?

—Lisa Carol Fremont: *Rear Window*

[YOU] HAVE TO GO.

—Gilbert Grape: *What's Eating Gilbert Grape*

[YOU'VE] GOT
THE SAME CHANCE
AS ANYONE ELSE.

—Charlie: *Willy Wonka and the Chocolate Factory*

YOU'VE BEEN GIVEN A GREAT GIFT.

—Clarence: *It's a Wonderful Life*

DON'T GIVE A HANG.

—Dallas: *The Outsiders*

[IT'S TIME TO] HAVE AN OLD FRIEND [OVER] FOR DINNER.

—Dr. Hannibal Lecter: *The Silence of the Lambs*

THAT'S AN ORDER.

—Admiral T.J. Cassidy: *Top Gun*

SIMPLY REMEMBER
[YOUR] FAVORITE THINGS.

—Maria: *The Sound of Music*

BE ON YOUR GUARD.

—Mrs. Baumer:
All Quiet on the Western Front

GO ONE MOMENT MORE.

—Karen: *Out of Africa*

YEAH, WHY NOT?

—James Bond: *Goldfinger*

IT WILL PROTECT YOU.

—Renfield's Mother: *Dracula*

IT'S ENOUGH.

—Hobson: *Arthur*

IT'S A BIG STEP FORWARD.

—Jim: *Days of Wine and Roses*

BRAVO, BRAVO.

—Alan Swann: *My Favorite Year*

[YOU] CAN FIX THAT.

—Hubbell: *The Way We Were*

THINGS COULD BE BETTER.

—Jack Torrance: *The Shining*

DON'T LET ANYONE
TALK YOU OUT OF IT.

—Julia: *Julia*

ANYTHING ABOUT IT SEEM UNUSUAL TO YOU?

—Agent K: *Men in Black*

[YOU'VE GOT]
ALL THE TIME IN THE WORLD
TO THINK ABOUT IT.

—Ellis Boy "Red" Redding:
The Shawshank Redemption

[YOU ARE] JUST INCHES
FROM A CLEAN GETAWAY.

—Garrett Breedlove: *Terms of Endearment*

THIS MEANS SOMETHING.

—Roy Neary: *Close Encounters of the Third Kind*

ABSOLUTELY.

—Agent J: *Men in Black*

YOU JUST GOTTA
SEE YOURSELF MAKIN' IT.

—Paula: *An Officer and a Gentleman*

WAITING [WON'T BE] YOUR IDEA OF THE KING OF INDOOR SPORTS.

—Jerry: *The Divorcee*

YOU KNOW WHAT YOU GOTTA DO, COWBOY.

—Joe Buck: *Midnight Cowboy*

I THINK IT PISSES GOD OFF
[IF] YOU WALK BY [IT]
AND DON'T NOTICE.

—Shug: *The Color Purple*

THE ANSWER'S OUT THERE SOMEWHERE.

—Lieutenant John Harper: *Plan 9 from Outer Space*

WHO COULD ASK
FOR ANYTHING MORE?

—Jerry Mulligan: *An American in Paris*

YES.

—Auntie Mame Dennis: *Auntie Mame*

IT [COULD] MAKE THINGS A MESS.

—Ronny Cammareri: *Moonstruck*

[DON'T] BE SENTIMENTAL.

—John "Scottie" Ferguson: *Vertigo*

STICK TO FICTION.

—Valesco: *The Third Man*

FLAUNT IT, BABY, FLAUNT IT!

—Max Bialystock: *The Producers*

[IT] IS LIKE MANURE.
IT'S NOT WORTH A THING
UNLESS [YOU]
SPREAD [IT] AROUND.

—Dolly Levi: *Hello, Dolly!*

TEMPTATION RESISTED IS A TRUE MEASURE OF CHARACTER.

—Louis Dega: *Papillon*

YOU'LL FEEL BETTER IF YOU CAN SEE [IT].

—Jack Griffin: *The Invisible Man*

GET DOWN OFF THAT HORSE.

—Cole Thorton: *The Road to El Dorado*

[WHAT] YOU WERE LOOKING FOR [IS] TOO CLOSE.

—Walter Neff: *Double Indemnity*

HOW LONG CAN [IT] LAST?

—Rocky: *They Shoot Horses, Don't They?*

IF YOU LOOK FOR IT,
YOU CAN FIND SOMETHING GOOD.

—Lowenthal: *Ship of Fools*

THINGS [MIGHT] WORK OUT AWFUL FUNNY.

—Bud Stamper: *Splendor in the Grass*

GO AHEAD AND LAUGH.

—Fanny Brice: *Funny Girl*

YOU CAN MAKE IT.

—Rev. Frank Scott: *The Poseidon Adventure*

ACKNOWLEDGMENTS

This book is dedicated to my dear friend and movie-going companion Sandra E. Jones. She has persevered through the "good," the "bad," and the "ugly" but still looks forward to the opening and closing credits of each film. Sandra, even the bad films we've seen have been a pleasure with you. Thank you.

Oscar-sized thank-yous to my movie friends: Heidi Andersen, Barbara Brownstein, Hanna Burns, Kris Caldwell, Peg Caldwell, Billie Condon, Bob Cumbow, Renee Erickson, Tim Gabor, Bill & Elaine Grace, Shannon Haider, Elke Hermann, Britta Hendren, Keith & Jean, Donni Kennedy, Jennifer Lang, Maureen McLaughlin, Jeffry Mitchell, Victoria Sanders, Pat Takayama, Diana Taylor and Janet Yoder.

AUTHOR'S NOTE

Researching *The Movie Book of Answers*® was a wonderfully large chal-
lenge. My first question was: What films to include? What better place to
go for the answer than to the original *Book of Answers*®? From it I received
YES. *The Literary Book of Answers*®' reply was Elizabeth Barrett Browning's
COUNT THE WAYS. So to push my own selection bias I started asking people
around me: What are your favorite films? What a cross-section I got! Now
I had to find about 325 quotes that would express something about that
film and work to answer a question.

There are many films that I watched simply because they are synonymous
with growing up in this "Hollywood" culture: *The Wizard of Oz, Snow
White and the Seven Dwarfs, It's a Wonderful Life* and *The Sound of Music.*
Then there are the films that are big to the culture. Their cinematogra-
phy, poignancy and the public's reaction to them, Hollywood has tried to
duplicate many times over: *Citizen Kane, Casablanca, Gone with the Wind,
Psycho, The Magnificent Seven, Apocalypse Now, Do the Right Thing, Close
Encounters of the Third Kind, King Kong* and *2001: A Space Odyssey.* Next
are the films that are put in the "cult classics" department of the video
store: *What Ever Happened to Baby Jane?, The Rocky Horror Picture Show,
A Clockwork Orange, Victor/Victoria* and *Night of the Living Dead.*

All that said, two things remained the same throughout this process: the
excitement that people expressed when they recalled their favorite

movies; and the idea that as a species our struggles, joys and fears remain powerfully similar. Films have continued to be a form of expression that remind us how much a part of a much larger world we are and what a thrill it can be to see it through another person's eyes, even for 120 minutes.